T0157186

QUEBEC

CORRUPTION

QUEBEC
CORRUPTION

VERONICA LA GENTILE

QUEBEC CORRUPTION

iUniverse books may be ordered through booksellers or by contacting:

iUniverse
1663 Liberty Drive
Bloomington, IN 47403
www.iuniverse.com
844-349-9409

ISBN: 978-1-6632-4449-9 (sc)
ISBN: 978-1-6632-4450-5 (e)

Print information available on the last page.

iUniverse rev. date: 08/23/2022

Introduction

This is a summary in english of a legal denunciation called "Quebec corruption" posted all over the medias where I explain with proof by documents of a fraud that I have been victim of by a financial institution in Quebec. In allowing this fraud a cover-up started from a notary and a supposed partner member of the financial institution and their employees from the legal system right up to all levels of two governments. All this to protect this financial institution not to be charged of money laundering, in my case, stealing my house and money and selling a stolen good to the accused in a criminal court case for proceed of crime

A copy of the french denunciation has been sent with all documents as proof and names of each corrupted person involved to our Prime Minister François Legault, to the minister of justice Simon Jolin-Barette and to Geneviève Guilbault minister of public security.

It has taken me more then 30 years to finally get my whole proof and what I have lived in that time is a horror story that we could never imagine or expect to live in a civilized world. That is the reason why I want the whole world to know this. Giving up was never an alternative because thousands of people in Quebec like we were victims of this financial institution. The difference with me was that I had the money to fight them, the education having studied for a bachelor in arts, political science and even went to law school. I also never all my life took no for an answer if I knew I was right.

I send a copy of my book with the names of every person involved in this fraud with full proof to the ministers of this governments because all along the crown blocked my case and didn't want to do any accusations or collaborate in any way to the point of stopping the police to do accusations consequently the department of fraud of the S.Q. did serious illegalities to stop me from trying to get justice.

I had no choice but to go public because having all my proof I have intentions of doing a private claim in criminal court. I think that the crown would try again to stop me by refusing to do accusations again.

By going public the two past governments are blamed publicly for having covered up and ordered every level of their government to stop my case knowing i had all my proof. My case would therefore serve of proof of all the other cases that never got justice. The thing to do is stop me in any way to get to the end of my case so that the financial institution would be protected and so I would not be the proof for all the other cases. This will all be proven in this document.

A View on My Life

At the age of four I started to figure skate and being competitive in that sport was my dream. I was very successful won many competitions and medal trophies having the chance to have the best teacher in the world.

Mr Gustavo Lussi trained me in New York and all the best skaters from all countries and therefore I made many friends from all over the planet. Many of them I kept in touch with.

When i was in law school I was offered to started a figure skating center of four ice rinks in Brossard (QC), the idea enchanted me of thinking of the chance the kids would have to be able to train all those hours each days. So I worked really hard in starting the first "Sport-étude" program in Quebec so all skaters could go to school during half of the days and skate for the rest of the time. I then contacted all my friends i skated with in my youth and all my other contacts. In two years the four rinks were full all day long. It was a real success that the owners were very impressed with and truthfully so was I.

Many skaters came from all over and so did teachers. They all needed to be lodged. Having inherited from a big amounted of money from my father's sister and from my father and having a big amount of my own I decided to build a big house to lodge whoever wanted to come live at my house. The house was like a big Italian villa with nine big rooms six bathrooms and a big dorm downstairs. In little time, the house got filled with skaters, teachers and even junior major hockey players. In the summer I even had more than forty in the house from players at the hockey schools at the rinks.

The person who sold me my land came up with a great idea. He suggested me to sell my house and build in the back on his 30 acres. He suggested to build my house attached to a big lodge since he was the president of the social cultural exchanges of Quebec. He then could lodge 4000 people all in one location and this would be going on every year. The proposition was great and it all could be done because of the great employees working for me who were very excited with the idea. Skaters junior majors and teachers offered to help.

I put the house for sale and two weeks laters a lady came to offer me my price leaving me to take all my chandeliers from my parent's house imported from Italy and my toilet accessories also from Italy of great value. Her only condition was that I go shopping with her to help her replace them.

A little later two inspectors of the government came at the door asking me to make of my house an elderly home and add an extension to lodge 48 people because they had to close three centers in very bad conditions. I was very reluctant to the idea but after taking me to see one of the center I was very upset to see these poor old people living in such bad condition. Knowing how busy I was they suggested that I take three partners each at 25% of the shares to make a $500 000 extension for a $100 000 project. They told me since I was on a one and only land getting the permit would not be a problem. I told them I had to speak to my branch manager because he has been a great friend who helped me build my house and I never made any financial decision without him approving of it. So I did and he thought it was a fantastic idea, that he would help me all the way and he proved to me that the income of the residence for elderly would pay for my two mortgages and more. So having such a positive opinion from him and knowing he would support me all the way, I was a bit more confortable with the idea.

My First Supposed Partner

The next morning at 5:30 in the morning I was having my coffee before getting on the ice when the mother of one of my boys I was teaching for almost two years asked me why I looked so preoccupied. I told her my situation and she being an analyst for C.B.C. right away offered to be a partner, she said that she would do all the business part of it even suggested to change to her branch of Radio-Canada (C.B.C) because she had been dealing with that manager for more than ten years and she could get any loan wanted from him. She also said she could get a loan on her house from her manager to buy half of my house, take half of my mortgage and we each could find a partner to invest in the other half of the building. She also told me that this chance came at the right time for her because her husband lost his job teaching at a college because of his accent, the pupils could not understand him well.

That evening my second partner and her husband Robert, parents of one of my pupils living in my house showed up to see their daughter. Over a coffee I informed them of my project. They immediately asked to be partners owning two Metros (grocery store in QC) they said their contribution would be to provide us with all the food at a good price.

So I had already my two partners. The next morning at the rink I informed my first supposed partner, she was very happy but insisted on her being the first to invest because of all the work involved in the financial part of it and that she had a notary in mind who was a good friend of her branch manager that she also had been doing business with for years. Louise and her husband didn't mind so we proceeded to make her my first partner.

At that time I found out that my branch manager had a promotion at the first level of the financial institution and he didn't recommend me to deal with the one replacing him. After meeting with him I didn't want to have anything to do with him and as a vengeance he didn't take my mortgage out of my credit line as he was told to buy my former manager who also told me to take my money out of there. Coming back from Calgary I found out that he didn't take my mortgage from my credit line as he was told by my manager and after six weeks put a 60 days on my house. When I told my supposed first partner she immediately contacted her manager and set an appointment to open up a joint commercial bank account in which all transactions of the company were to be done and no other account. We met with the responsable person of mortgage who did all the documents necessary on the October 16th 1990.

The Visit at the Notary – Act of Sale

It was then that everything started and turned into the biggest nightmare of my life. On the October 25th of 1990 we had an appointment at her notary to sign an act of sale of half of my house for $112 500 and we both would pick up $112 500 of mortgage. The full mortgage being $225 000. I wanted to know how my mortgage passed from $195 000 to $225 000. He was very vague and said he had to see that all expenses were paid for. He never quite explained what else. Then saying he had not the time to read the whole act of sale he came to the part of "PRICE" saying that this sale was made for $112 500 that the amount was paid one part today and part before. He didn't have a check of $112 500 to give me and his act said he gave me the money. So of course I didn't want to sign it. His excuse was that he would pay me later, that he had many documents to make in very little time and his job as a notary is to make sure each investor is satisfied and treated impartially and that if I am not satisfied at the end I can sew him. The argument went on for quite a while and my supposed partner started to cry. Having had an uncle that was a notary I knew that often documents are done separately and the important thing is at the end all is balanced to the satisfaction of the parties involved. I signed but I was left with a bad feeling out of there. On the December 3rd 1990 Louise, my second partner, told him that she would buy only 10% of the shares from me and the other 15% when he pays me the $112 500 he owed me. He was fine with that so he gave me a check of $50 000 from Louise for 10% of $500 000. The next morning December 4th at 5:45, my first partner was at the rink asking me a check of $22 500 amount that she also would deposit in our business account for us to get the loan to start the extension of the building. She also asked me a check of $2 875 for my part of the expenses she had to do for the company and $ 1 600 for Louise's part that I should collect from her when I saw her. All of which had to go in our business account. It was understood that I would do a transaction at the end of each month from my branch in St-Luc into our business account to pay my part of the mortgage of $1 400. The first month went well but when it came to the end of December 1990, the deposit didn't go through and the cashier after calling the branch of Radio-Canada told me to go to that branch because the person that answered her told her that there had been a change of account that an other commercial account for our company had been opened illegally by my partner and my check of $22 500 was in that new account.

I hurried downtown to the branch when I walked in the girl that had opened our joint account rush to tell me to leave, that I couldn't talk to the manager and that my first partner had every right to open that account. I started to scream treating her of a liar and telling her that she knew right from the start that the account she opened for our company was to be the only one. I created a real show and she had me taking out of the branch by two men. She refused to give me any information and told me to speak to my partner.

I returned there one more time and was kicked out again, called the manager at least two or three times a day and he never called me back.

Louise and I went to the notary's office and he wouldn't let us come in his office, so we just pushed his office door open. He said he didn't have any documents that my partner had all the documents. We knew that was a lie a big fight went on and his secretary came in and said she would call the police. I said do, we need them. Finally we left I telling him "You don't remember anything anymore well when I am done with you, you won't forget me for the rest of your life!"

I Called Economical Crimes of the S.Q.

The next day I called the "Sûreté du Quebec" at economical crimes and was lucky enough to get an investigator who told me he had been trained by my dad who had been director of criminal researches for more than 20 years.

We right away connected and discussed by my situation he told me I am not the only one in this situation that there was many complaints in the department. He said not only the branch doesn't want to give us our file to provide us with documents necessary for our proof and defence but the crown so far has refuse to do a court order to get file from the different branches involved. However he said he was going to go to the crown and if he refuses he will try with a judge from the "Justice of peace". In fact, he had to go to the justice of peace judge and only got some documents from the branch. He got the read out of the new account opened illegal by my supposed partner, a list of checks made mostly to her name that she used for personal reasons, the company registration that said we were two in it, but at "ADMINISTRATORS" the notary said I lived at the address of my supposed partner when in the act of sale he lists me living at my home address. With that it was clear that it was fraud but we needed to have all the proof. The branch employee that gave him the documents told my investigator that my supposed partner was more than a friend of the manager and that for a long time.

Complaint at the Financial Institution

My investigator told me to put in a complaint in Quebec city so that the inspectors would go and get my file at the branch and also told me to get a lawyer. I called financial institution and got an inspector who told me that cases like mine are falling down like rain all over Quebec that the branches are robbing people of their houses, businesses, restaurants, gas stations and more. It's all fraud and in every case at the base of all the frauds there is always a lawyer and or a notary working for that financial institution. People can't get their documents to defend themselves and the crown refuses to intervene to court order the branches for them to get their files. The crown sends them to civil until they are washed out of money and their cases just die out.

The inspector after talking for long asked me if I had money to fight them I told them I had more than a half million from inheritance in a bank in an other city to my name and more from all my years of work. They asked me if I was willing to fight them after getting my file they will do anything for me to get to the end and try to be proof for others all across Quebec that lost everything. So we had a deal one that I was not ever to give up on.

As understood I called back two weeks later and the one that I spoken to after getting my file told me everything I needed to know. The notary was at the base of the fraud he was the instigator along with my first lawyer whom I had studied political science with whom I thought was a friend.

My First Lawyer

When I saw him at the office I had only the act of sale that said I had been payed so reading the act he said it was clear that he would do a deposition of fault of the act to get my supposed partner off the titles so I could sell my shares to an other person. But looking at the name of the notary at the end of the document his face fell to the floor. I asked him if he knew him he said not really from the time I was on the board of the Brossard branch but I am not anymore because I am too busy.

It so turned out that he still was on the board and pleaded for that branch being automatically in conflict of interest in taking my case. My supposed partner being informed by him and the notary of my actions took us to court to put a "sequester" to impound my house and I then found out that my lawyer instead of doing a deposition of fault of the act of sale, did a procedure to say that i was not paid, which left her still with her name on my property. The judge was furious and said I had rights against him for not having done the right procedure. Later I found out that he and the notary were running the branch of Brossard illegally with a "Back office" under the direction of the president of the first level of Montreal. So now I had to find an other lawyer because I didn't want to pay him having done the wrong procedure but he put a lean on my house so I had to pay him.

The Chase for a New Lawyer

I must of seen more than six lawyers trying to get one to plead my case. All of them after studying the file or just knowing that it was against that institution refused and said they wanted nothing to do with them and their frauds and they didn't want to be pressured or bought off by them.

Finally after paying $2 800 of mortgage imposed by the branch of Radio-Canada to stay in my house and never getting a call or being able to reach the manager I decides to stop paying. My supposed partner was nowhere to be seen and only payed one month of her part of the mortgage. I knew from my investigator there was still money in the account opened illegally and that was my money. So when the manager called after having been stopped from entering in my house by my house keeper, because i wasn't there, he refused to give me any information and said he would kick me out of it if I didn't pay. I told him to pay himself with my money in the new account thinking there was still some left, at that time I didn't know that the account had totally been emptied and he of course didn't say. He just said that if I didn't pay he would kick me out of my big Italian villa.

Knowing this I had to find a lawyer right away.

I was recommended to one by a notary who said he didn't think he would take the case but said he was a bit nuts and would find the reason why the branch didn't want to give me my file or my information. In fact he was right he didn't want to plead against them but when I told him I couldn't get my information he asked me the phone number of that branch and asked to speak to the person responsable of commercial accounts. He started to scream at him asking him why I couldn't have my files, he told him he would have him picked up by the police if he didn't speak. Louise and I were laughing to tears but the employee crashed and told him there was a social reason in the file signed only by my supposed partner and made by the notary saying that my supposed partner was alone in the company, that it was fraud and the branch went along with it. Furious he told him that same notary declared us two in the company registration and it should have been a "banking resolution" signed by all investors to give her the rights to open up an other company account. The lawyer told him to have a copy ready at the reception desk in the morning at 9 O'clock, that my investigator would be there to pick it up and if it is not there it's him that they were going to pick up.

However, this lawyer refused to plead against the institution saying that i would be kicked out of my house like the people in Germany in the second world war and they would take all my money. He also told me no matter how much money I had that I would spend it all trying to get justice because they are protected by the government in power since they are their financial institution for their projects and financial help. He was right all the way and 30 years later I still think of him how honest he was.

Finally he pleaded my other case, the one of the bricklayer who wanted to buy my house and when I refused to sell it to him, he charged me an other $20 000 for the job. But he lost in court and the lawyer made him admit that he was trying to steal me of $20 000 because I didn't want to sell my house to him. The judge couldn't stop laughing.

The Second Lawyer

At the end one lawyer gave me the name of a lawyer that he said would probably take it because he would do anything for money. He was right this lawyer took it but wanted $10 000 in cash to represent me if I got a 60 days days from the branch and to ask the judge for a court order to the branch so I could have my file to be able to defend myself.

I brought it right away to him but when the court day came he didn't show up in court and the branch took possession of my house by default. I made a scene at him and told him I held him responsable if I lost my house. He then sent a letter to all levels of the institution but it didn't change a thing because the lawyer of the first level of the institution said that his boss the president of the Montreal first level wanted $2 800 from me and a letter saying I wouldn't sew them but I refused.

On the 18th of May 1993 I got kicked out of my house. At 8 O'Clock in the morning North American van line was at my door with a bailiff. My hockey players call the St-Luc police who knew about my situation visiting often some of my players and going to see their hockey games. One police said not to open the door until they got there. The bailiff had a judgement signed by the private lawyer of the president of the first level. I found that out by the president of the victims of the institution who had a website denouncing more than 100 cases including mine and having made many articles in the newspapers. Those articles are sent to François Legault, Simon Jolin-Barrette and Geneviève Guilbault along with naming all the criminals involved.

Realizing that I was probably right the bailiff decided to close the door after taking all my kitchen and living room outside. He was also shocked that the boss of North American van lines told his employees on the phone not to load the truck, to leave everything on the side of the road because it was probably an other fraud of that financial institution and he didn't want to have anything to do with that anymore.

So all my belongings were left there in the house and the bailiff said that if its fraud the institution will have to give me back my house and all my belongings in my house.

I had to leave and rent a house in Brossard to lodge some of my boarders and most of the rest of them were placed in an other pension by their association.

It was a devastating situation and the boys even called le Journal de Montreal and an article past the next day in which the manager said he kicked me out because I didn't pay my mortgage for a long time. How degenerate can anyone be?

I then contacted financial institutions and my investigator having see the article in the paper decided to go and see his boss the chef inspector with my file and many other to ask him permission to go and see a judge in superior court to ask him to put out an injonction for all the branches in each of his cases to give us our file so we would have our proof to defend ourselves. He told me to call him back in one or two weeks.

So I did, and I was told by the secretary that he wasn't working there anymore. I was shocked. I needed to talk to him because my S.Q. investigator returned to the crown with the fraudulent social reason made by the notary saying that my supposed partner was alone in the company and in the company registration he declares that we are two (Louise had not bought her shares at that time) The crown told my investigator that he would do something if he had the extract of resolution of the opening of the second account without me knowing.

I called back financial institution and asked to speak to the other investigator who went to the branch of Radio-Canada to get my file. He took my call and was furious telling me that the next day his partner went to ask the chief inspector for a permission to go and make an injonction in a superior court judge he was called back in his office to be dismissed from his job. He said I have your file on my desk what do you need to know I will tell you everything you need. I told him I had to have the extract of resolution of the second account of company opened without me knowing. He said the extract? There are two, something that has never been seen. In the first one on the 23th of November 1990 your partner says she is the president of the company you are the vice- president and her husband is an administrator and he has never been registered in the company. The 18th of February 1991 there is an other extract saying she is alone in the company just as the social reason says at paragraph 5th that she is alone in the company and she only sign it. Yet in the registration of the company the same notary says you are two in the company. You can't have more false documents than that even if you try.

Now he said I am going to give you the phone number of the right-hand of the president of the financial institution because you won't get to speak to the president, he hides behind his right-hand and makes him do all the dirty work. You will tell him that you need the two extracts, that I told you everything in your file and that he needs to make you a copy and also that the police needs to pick up the documents in 48 hours. If not, he will be picked up by them.

So I did, he was furious and threatened me by saying "You will see what will happen to you if you don't stop harassing our institution" So I said treats I had them before twice saying I will get out of my house feet first if I didn't stop. Well, let me tell you I didn't and I won't. I also have a threat for you, I have the economical crimes on the other line and in 48 hours they are going to get the two extracts or you so you better make sure you have them ready for them. I could hear a voice in the back it had to be the voice of the president who does for sure hide behind him.

My Investigator Returned

When my investigator got them after coming to show them to me he returned to see the crown and showed them to him. All the crown wanted to hear was how he got them. He of course after a long fight with the investigator refused to do anything. So my investigator told him you wanted the extract of resolution I just brought you two for the same account. I also I have a social reason that should have been a "Banking resolution". In the social reason the notary says that she is alone in the company yet the same notary says that we are two in the registration papers of the company. That's not enough for you this isn't civil it's criminal and you know it. Furious the crown kicked him out of his office.

A few days later he called me and said he was taking his pension because all this work lead to nothing and because the crown blocks all cases against that institution and that is the case for all the investigators who have cases against that financial institution.

My file passed to one other investigator who told me what had happened in the office with my investigator when the crown refused to act. I felt bad for him so I decided to take an appointment with the crown to confront him since I had law knowledge. For at least 25 minutes proving him all the fraud points he kept telling me it was a civil case and I told him "I see, well it looks like we didn't study the same criminal code, I will leave now and will go rob a branch of that institution it will be a faster way to pay myself back. However when and if the cops try to arrest me I will send them to you so you can explain to them that it isn't criminal it's civil!" He was screaming like a fool in a mad rage.

The Civil Parade

In 1991 my supposed partner took us to court, put an impound on the house. My first lawyer having done the wrong procedure the judge had to put one on the house.

In 1992 with my second lawyer we did a procedure to ask permission with the act of sale to be heard in a court because I wasn't paid and the act says I was, the judge in 10 minutes read the part of the act that said I was paid turned around and asked for a receipt or a check to prove I was paid. After hesitation the lawyer of the notary said she didn't have one. So the judge said that there will be a hearing because the act says clearly that I was paid.

In 1995 the hearing. It was a real joke. The notary and my first partner said I sold my house for half the mortgage because I was out of money. Which was a lie. The lawyer of my partner showed a false little paper saying that the house was evaluated at $225 000 only, and the lies went on and on. Finally seeing that my lawyer didn't say anything I got up and ask after more then two hours, permission to speak.

I asked the judge if he had a house, he said yes, well did you get a loan of 100% on your house? He said no. I said I guess that like me you got a loan of 65% (at that time) He said yes So I said explain to me how the lawyer of my supposed partner can convince you that on my house I got a loan for $225 000 that is my full mortgage as explained by the notary. Also explain to me how the lawyer of my supposed partner can convince you that the little paper he has to prove that my house is evaluated at $225 000 is valid in court when I am sure you know that the only evaluation on a house accepted in court is the one of the financial institution and the one of the insurance? Third of all explain to me why the notary made an act of sale, which implies a money transaction when he says that because I had money problems I sold half of my house for only the half of the mortgage which he knows in that case he should have done an act of cession that is in english a transfer of half of the mortgage which does not involved any money transaction. I got all this information from the notarial board, if you check with them they will tell you the same. Finally if like me you got 65% of the value of your house for the mortgage, in my case my full value of my house would be $450 000. Now explain to me why I would sell my house for half the mortgage when legally I could ask my institution to raise my loan if I was in a tight financial situation. Also, to end it all, I had an other partner who wanted to buy the half and had the money, why would I sell to her first?

My lawyer kept telling me to sit down the judge was red in the face. The crowd was laughing and the judge got up and said that probably with more proof I will see the light on my case. So I answered "The light is here for one that doesn't want to close their eyes." I finished by saying that this whole morning was a real joke when the first judge that we asked to go in a hearing saw I wasn't paid and in no time at all, he declare the act as false.

The judge flew out of the room and my lawyer was furious saying I could be behind bars for that. Later on I found out why he didn't speak at the "plumitif" at the court house then we could ask for the cases a lawyer pleaded. I found out that later on that specific year of my case he was pleading three cases for that financial institution. He had been bought off for sure. So again I had to change lawyer. That also explained why he didn't want to sew the past lawyer for not having done the right procedure.

In 1994 I went to meet the person in charge of complaints at the highest level of the financial institution. I showed him all my proof that she had opened an other company account, the social reason that should have been a "Banking resolution" and the rest of the documents i had. Later on he answered me by letter saying that after checking with the branch my supposed partner had every right to open an other account. I knew right then by that answer he was covering up for the institution.

The Third Lawyer in 1996

It took me more than a year to find an other lawyer because of all the same reasons explained before, none of them wanted to go against that institution. After talking with him for a long time, I managed to convince him. He was a corporate lawyer who asked me $25 000 to court order the branch and interrogate the manager and his employees. However, the condition was that I didn't sew him if anything went wrong. I had no choice I needed a lawyer.

He did two court orders never got all the documents especially the mortgage act which was the most important to prove the fraud. He also was refused by their lawyer to interrogate the manager which was the main person to interrogate. I was interrogated first by their lawyer, a real scum with no respect who attacked me as if I was a criminal. Seeing my lawyer wasn't doing anything to stop him, I jumped at him, treating him of every word in the book.

He was stunned and admitted that it wasn't only the institution responsable of this fraud but there were two more involved. That he will send the proof to my lawyer with the rest of the documents asked.

He did, he sent the proof of my first lawyer who started the whole fraud and the proof of the notary, but never sent the mortgage act. He also told my lawyer he would ask the institution to settle me if not he was getting out of the file. He did get out because the institution never wanted to settle me.

My lawyer did procedure against every level of the institution and the second lawyer. However which was very strange to me he advised me to drop the charges against my second lawyer, saying I had to keep my money to go against the institution who was the real responsable of the fraud. I found it strange. But later on by an other lawyer I heard that he pleaded more than one time for the bar association, which would explain why he suggested me not to sew the second lawyer. He also closed his eyes on the fraud of the notary putting all the responsibility on the branch not giving me my information. An other point that shocked me was the social reason being a corporate lawyer he had to have known that the notary was at the bottom of the whole fraud. But he was always evasive when I brought that up. So I started to have doubts about him which later on proved to be right. He never registered his procedure in court.

Louise's Husband Made An Offer on My House

A few months after I got kicked out of my house, Louise's husband made an offer on my house. I never received any documents from the branch at my house in two and half years but in June 1993, one month after being put out of my house, one day going to check my mailbox, I got a document from the Radio-Canada branch saying that the balance to pay on my house was $240 000. How could that be $15 000 more than the initial mortgage after I had been paying $2 800 a month for two and a half years? Robert, then decides to go to his manager in Sherrington and make a notarial offer as being first offering. $240 000 so I could get my house back. That meant that the branch could not sell it to anyone without contacting that notary if they had an offer.

In 1997 I saw my house on the news, seized for proceeds of crime by the R.C.M.P.

It was on T.V.A. (Quebec broadcast) the institution past over Robert's offer and sold it to the accused by money laundering. I immediately called the investigator and was lucky enough to get him before court. He was shocked and asked me if it was really my house. I said of course, i built it with the architect. He then said he was going to court with the case and couldn't tell me anything but he referred me to the investigator of "Carcajou" who seized the house with him who also had the total file and would help me since the branch never gave me my proof in total necessary at criminal.

The Investigator of "Carcajou"

This person was the best thing that happened to me, he told me everything one document at a time. He told me that the notary was at the bottom of the whole fraud and directed the whole fraud. He said the reason why the lawyer of the branch didn't provide us with the mortgage act is because it is the most important document and so are the titles at the registration office are. It so happens that it was an "identity fraud" the notary in the titles put my house in the mortgage act registration to the name of my supposed partner on the 23th of October and two days later in the act of sale I sell her half of my house why? Like he said on the 23th of October she is already the only owner of your house, you are not there anymore. That is why he gave her a social reason saying at paragraph 5 that she is alone in the company operating at your house that is now hers. You were paying $2 800 per month for a house that belong to her. That is why in May 1992 as you said to me she came with two other persons broke in to tell you to get out it was her house. Lucky for you one of the hockey player came to say to go because the police was on their way, he called them.

He also asked me if I was there on the 23th of October 1990 when the mortgage act was signed. I said of course not,

I only saw the notary for the first time on the 25th when we went for the act of sale. Well he said we figured it out, did he make you sign documents on the 25th of October?I said yes very fast he pulled out papers and made me sign saying it was for the branch like insurance etc. Well he said, one was the sheet of signature of the act of mortgage that he them took to go and change it from the one he registered the act of mortgage on the 24th of October.

I will prove it to you the mortgage act was signed on the 23th of October 1990 and registered on the 24th the next day which is usually the case, but if you look at the act of sale it was registered only on the 29th of October, four days after the signature of the act which is not normal. So it means that on the 25th of October after he made you sign the signature sheet of of the mortgage act without you knowing he then the next day on the 26th of October went to change de sheet of the mortgage act that he registered on the 24th for the new one that has your signature. So he then returned on the 29th to register the act of sale, that is four days after the document was signed, that is not normal, documents are usually registered one to two days after the signatures are done maximum.

I couldn't believe it but he told me that he has been doing that job for more than 20 years and has seen it all in fraud for him and the team it was easy to figure out that I wasn't there to sign the mortgage act on the 23th of October 1990. He helped me for more than a year to figure out all my documents and told me what next to do and said to call him anytime.

After figuring all my documents with me he told me to consult a criminal firm of defendants and inform myself of which was one of the best ones. I did and one of the owners and his researcher met with me took the case and said they would contact me in a month to tell me what they found.

At The Criminalist Firm in 1999

They called me back then called in two of of economical crimes investigators of the S.Q. and my civilist who didn't want to come to the meeting but was told if he didn't they would send someone special to escort him. The owner of the firm explained the whole fraud to them and gave them the documents to go to the crown and tell him he sent them. He then told my civilist to hurry to go and get the acts declared false because at civil we have very little time, it's 10 years and we are on the 9th year.

The police were waiting for me downstairs to give me back the documents saying that it was useless to go back to the crown that he refuses to act against that institution. The next day my civilist called me and said to come and get my file that he wanted nothing to do with that criminal firm and he on top of it wanted $600 for copies of the court order documents. I couldn't believe it, the criminal firm was right, there was no way he didn't see the fraud especially that the notary did a "Social reason" instead of a "Banking resolution". The criminalist asked him many questions putting him on a spot like why he didn't ask for the mortgage act in his court orders. The explanation was that he felt caught by the criminal firm and wanted out of the file knowing who he had to deal with.

I called back the investigator of "Carcajou"

The criminal firm told me to go and get the acts on my supposed partner's house to see if she really did make a loan to pay me. The investigator of "Carcajou" also suggested me to do so the last time I talked to him.

From 1993 to 1999

After I got kicked out of my house I never stopped harassing the branch, the first level and the top level of the institution for my file to get my full proof of the fraud. I got two threats to my life during that time and the police told me to leave for an other province because they knew I had the money to fight them and I was a threat to them that this whole diabolic cover up would be discovered and be the proof for others that didn't have the money nor legal knowledge or guts to confront them.

At that time I was on 4 pills a day having been diagnosed with PTSD (Post Traumatic Stress Disorder) by Health Quebec and was on disability in Quebec. I never got over having to leave my house with all my belongings left there all my souvenirs and all my family belongings that my mother gave me after she sold her house and she died from the shock. In other words all their lifetime goods including mine, my medals and trophies of all my skating carrer even my last pair of skates and competition dresses.

I also had $30 000 of jewellery accumulated from my parents and family over the years. All the equipment to lodge 40 people was also left there. The only thing that was put out by North American Van Line was the kitchen and living room. All was left in the street because their boss didn't want them to load the vans since it was an other fraud of that financial institution. The only transportation we were able to get was a hay wagon from a farmer and all my expensive dishes were broken to pieces when we opened up the boxes. A lot were very expensive imports from Italy. My silver was also left behind all the Louis XV table setting and tea and coffee in silver on a big silver plates. I never got over loosing all my life memories, it seemed to me like they were trying to erase my whole life, and I promised myself never to stop to get justice and denounce those criminals until the day I die.

I got to Ontario in 1999 and the doctor I saw sent me to a great specialist on the board of Health Canada. He was great, took me off all those pills I ended up with only two that he prescribed me and told me to be patient that it would take me at least 10 years before I get out of this shock. Thanks to him, today I am fine however I am on two pills for the rest of my life. It did take me that long to get back to a normal life but all along I never stopped trying every day to get justice.

In 1999

That year was a big year for me. It started by a phone call from an other victim of the financial institution, thanks to the president of the victims of the institution we were a group of about six of us keeping in touch trying to help each other. I was lucky enough that the president sent me all the articles that passed in the papers and most of the articles including mine that he wrote on the internet denouncing the institution.

This person said that he went to get the law of the financial institution in question and didn't understand that all the articles at every level of the institution it says that if you have a problem with one level, "you can" complain to each of the other two to get your problem solved. He said that all over it says "can" yet no level does anything to help us and solve our problem. Having some law knowledge I said it's impossible it shouldn't be "can" but "must" because it is a law voted by the National Assembly and laws are made to protect the citizens not to give a choice to the financial institution to solve our problem or not.

He insisted and offered to bring me the law for me to read it I did and he was right. I finally got to article 516 at two in the morning and I realized that the provincial government gives itself the power to judge of criminal infractions and at article 529 the penalty is fines which is civil. How can number one the provincial government give itself the right to judge of criminal infraction when only the federal has the unique power to judge criminal infraction and they are to be judge in criminal court. The infractions were all of fraud from article 517 to 529 like false inscription, refusing to inscribe, refusing to inform etc. All fraud articles that the crown has to act for the citizen being a victim of such infractions. Further more, only the federal government has the right to legislate when it comes to criminal infractions.

For a moment I thought I wasn't reading right but early in the morning I realized I was right and asked an immediate appointment with the criminal law firm. Both the criminalist and his researcher were shocked and said that with that I had the proof of why the crown doesn't act and why he sends everybody to civil. The law is unconstitutional, it doesn't respect the criminal code for one the provincial government is responsable for writing a law that doesn't respect the criminal code and second the federal is responsable for having given them a license to practice that doesn't respect the criminal code. They even pulled out a law case in jurisprudence to prove it and sent me to meet the minister of constitution at federal.

When I presented the whole thing to him he was shocked and told me I was right. he made me send my proof and file to the federal but told me to complain to the minister of justice at provincial the one who sold my house instead of giving it back to me as said the judgement in criminal court.

The criminal firm told me that the federal who was liberal at the time would not do anything because the unconstitutional law was voted by a provincial liberal government in 1961-1962 and was also given a license by a liberal federal government. The thing is that at federal all of them being english just never saw the flaw in the law. They also told me that it had to be a plan by the provincial liberal at the time because they were furious at the federal constantly crying injustice from the federal to Quebec.

Again in 1999

Now that i had all my proof I decides to go and confront a second time the person responsable of complaints at the top level of the institution.

When I showed him all my proof he was shocked and admitted it was fraud and that the manager was for sure under this whole thing because nothing in a branch happens without him knowing because he has to answer for all that happens in his branch. He also told me that for the manager my supposed partner was definitely more than a friend for him to risk his career for such a fraud. He told me that he would meet with his two superiors and ask them to settle me. I told him about the threats I got from the right arm of the president and he assured me they would settle me.

Later, not having news from him I contacted him and with a shaking voice he told me he tried everything and they just don't want to pay me.

In 1999 I called to inform my investigator of "Carcajou" who was happy to hear from me and asked me if I was back in my house. I said no, why? He was in every state of mind telling me that there is a judgment at criminal against the accused on my house and the judge says that she sent me a memo to come and claim my house in court. I told him I never got it and he said you should have your address is all over civil in court. Furious, he told me that the investigator of the R.C.M.P. pleaded identity fraud. That my house was stolen from me by a notary of the financial institution who put my house to the name of my supposed partner in the mortgage act, that the branch stole my house from me and sold a stolen good to the accused who bought it probably not knowing they bought a stolen house and were charged for it. He also told me that I should call the crown and confront him to ask him why he didn't call me to tell me to go claim my house in court because he got the judgment, his secretary signed it in the back. He said to call him back and he himself would make some calls.

I confronted the crown and asked him why he didn't call to tell me to go and claim my house. He wasn't talking and suddenly he screamed "I won't do any accusations against that financial institution, is that clear?" and he hung up on me. I called back my investigator of "Carcajou" the next day telling him he was disgusted and informed me that the minister of justice sold it very fast for $180 000 a house worth $450 000 on the market, then he told me that her job was to find me and give me back my house but she must of been told by the crown and the government to sell it fast because there was already a blocked offer on it and they didn't want me to discover the fraud that the institution did to me when I would have gotten it back. The crown didn't want to let me know because in the judgment the judge says that her job in this case is to judge only the proceeds of crime part not the lawsuit before it nor after it. That is not for her to judge my fraud which was pleaded by the R.C.M.P. to prove that my house was stolen from me and also not for her to judge the lawsuit after proceeds of crime which was the fact that the financial institution had laundered money. And that is why the crown said he would not accuse the financial institution because by accusing the branch in my case automatically the institution is in money laundering and stealing my house and he just didn't want to do so, he had to protect the institution.

He had been put there to stop any accusations against the institution and that is also why the minister of justice at the time sold my house very quickly went over the offer of Robert and sold it for little money to the accused on my house by an other corrupted notary which I know the name.

2001-2002

A visit to the chef of cabinet of the party

Knowing all that, I decided to ask to meet the Prime Minister of Quebec at the time. But he passed me on to his lawyer chief of cabinet which was even better. When I got in I said "You are a lawyer aren't you"? He said yes well I asked him if he was aware of all the frauds of the Quebec financial institution. After hesitating a while he said yes, by the newspapers. So I explained all my case with proof by documents. He was shocked and asked me how I had all the money to get that far. I said Oh! I still have more to get to the end and then go public if I am not justified. But if I go public, then everybody gets justice. I asked him why his government didn't stop the institution He answered me because our hands are tied. Tied I said because the institution holds you in power by financing your party and your government projects am I right? He answered me by "You did your homework well!" I asked him if that was the reason he went 25to law school to see his people being framed all over Quebec, knowing about it and not standing up to do anything to stop them.

I also asked him if he had seen the article in the Journal de Montreal in 2000 where the president of the institution takes the president of the victims of the institution to court in slander for all his articles published on internet and in the papers. He said yes, well I said, in the article he says he was humiliated by the Prime Minister at the time and his minister of finance, who questioned him on the frauds of his institution. Are you surprised that the president of the institution sold out the two of them by this declaration, he declares that the two of them knew and we know nothing was done to stop him and force him to settle the people that were slandered. Consequently, the Prime Minister left his position after four years and left to go to his house in California. He knew very well that he was responsible for not doing anything to stop him. You as a lawyer you should know that if you are aware of a crime and do nothing to stop it, you automatically become an accomplice, just like you, you are in the same position!

An other point that went in the papers also is the fact that the president of the victims went to meet the passed Prime Minister from 1996 to 2000 and his minister of finance to ask permission to show to the National Assembly and expose his 100 cases of victims and he was refused and asked to leave. That is called covering up a crime that you are aware of.

He got really nervous and said he was going to personally do something about it. I left and said I should hope so for your sake because I can assure you I will get to the end of this if it means that I have to expose everyone. A little later, to my big surprise I saw him on television as a new member of the new federal party. Up to today I wonder if I had to do anything about it.

A Visit to See The Chief Supreme Court Judge of Canada

All my youth and forever this well known criminalist had been the dearest friend of my father. I was for years impressed and touched by the friendship they had. When he was named chief justice of Canada, my father was so happy, it was one of the times he was the most happy in his life, it made me realize what deep friendship they had. My friend from Montreal Germaine, knowing that and being in the association of "Justice for all" told me that I should go and see him so he can tell me what he thinks about my file. She knew him very well since he had been for years a member of the association for which she was president.

2003 Meeting with My Father's Dear Friend

It was in Ottawa at a law firm for which he was a consultant after his years of being a Chief Supreme court judge were over. It was a very emotional moment for both of us since I hadn't seen him since my dad died.

He told me that Germaine told him about my case and he was very upset and asked if it was possible for me to come and see him. I was very touched and he said that all this situation would not have happened to me if my father was alive, so it was his job now to guide me to the end.

He asked me for the acts and in a flash he had seen all the fraud of the notary in all his documents. He told me that this person was a very sick individual and for sure I wasn't the only one he frauded. He knew right away that the act of sale was contradictory by itself and also both acts contradicted themselves. For sure the manager was in on the whole situation and saw right away that the manager lent too much money to my supposed partner and his friend notary put my house to the name of my supposed partner to guarantee all the excess loans the manager did for her. He told me that if I got all the acts on her property it would be proven that she and the manager were in trouble. The manager for having given her all those loans and her for not having probably the money to pay them all. So putting my house to her name was a great opportunity for both of them because my house was half paid and she could take a loan on it if she needed more money which she did in 1991. I have the copy in my file showing that she took a loan on my house signed by the manager and the employee who we met to open the first joint account.

In such little time, he saw everything I was so impressed. He also said that the judge in 1995 in hearing on the act of sale had for sure been given instructions, he was part of the cover up since they saw I had money to keep on in civil. He strongly advised me to go in appeal of that judgment now that I had all my proof.

He said civil is 10 years it is expired but you will see what the judge will say now that you have all the proof. He will have to reject it because it is not civil it's a criminal case but he might be an honorable person and advise you honestly, which would be in your favour.

The L.R.2.C.4.1 Unconstitutional Law

He asked me if I had more to show him. I said yes, something that would make you fall off your chair. Showing him article 516 of the law of the institution and the articles of fraud turned into civil he was shocked and said that would this he has seen it all of Quebec. He asked me who discovered that flaw in the law. I said I did. When I saw that, the crown refused to help by court order all these people to get their proof and that he so arrogantly told me he would not accuse the financial institution I just had to know why and how he was so sure of himself in doing so. I told him about my friend getting the law and when I heard about the "Can" all over the law instead of "must" knowing it was a law that was supposed to protect the interest of the people since voted by the National Assembly I had to read it and that is how I got to article 516. The Government of Quebec gives itself the right to legislate in criminal when we knew that only the federal can do so in criminal matters. Then from article 517 to 529 all criminal offenses of fraud are sent to article 529 where the penalties are fines, in other words civil and that is why the crown sends everybody to civil. Having lost everything and money they can't last long in civil so the cases die out. But I had and still have money to keep on that is why I am driving everybody crazy and at all level now they are having to cover up so that I don't get to the end and have all the proof for everybody that they frauded. As if it's not enough, I have a judgment from criminal court pleaded by the R.C.M.P. where the judge say she sent me a "notice" to go claim my house because it was sold for proceeds of crime. I never got the notice and when I confronted the crown he told me he would not accuse the institution and hung up on me.

After seeing the judgment he said that there is already a judgment on my house, that my house was stolen from me by the notary's false documents and the proof of all that is that the accused are charged of being in possession of a stolen house. The proof is that when the institution took judgment on my house it was written to Veronica La Gentile and all. so that is the proof that the institution knew it was your house all the time and are complice to the fraud.

He told me that I will have to wait for the government to change because a federal liberal government will not do anything against a provincial liberal government, who in 1961-1962 by their jurists of the party wrote an unconstitutional law by revenge to the federal for feeling unjustly treated by the policies of the federal for a long time. However he said I don't think that they would imagine that 30 years later a president of a Quebec financial institution would use that flaw in the law with his lawyers and notaries in the institution, to fraud the people of Quebec.

This plan was well thought of in the case that a "YES" would be voted at the 1995 referendum. It was to steal as much people with money or valuable goods so they could have enough money (a financial cushion) to help the separatists party financially and have enough for their projects not needing monetary help from the federal. But that didn't happen so now the only thing to do is to cover up and stop any case to get out by any possible way. So that is how the cover up goes to all levels of the government and even to the next one after 1995 that will be elected to protect that Quebec financial institution so you are in for a big and long fight. When the federal government changes that will be the time to try and get that law repealed by the next Prime Minister of Canada who is a constitutionalist and will have great pleasure in doing so by his lawyers in his cabinet.

They will be very impressed as I am that you discovered that flaw in the law. All those years in your youth of reading the criminal code paid of, when all the girls of your age were reading romance you studied the criminal code from cover to cover. Your dad and I had a good laugh to see that and how well you knew it.

There is an other point I want to bring up is the fact that no matter what the politicians in Quebec try to separate the province from Canada, there is a law in the constitution in Canada that can be used to stop them. No province by constitution is separable from the others in Canada. If in 1995 at the referendum the people would have voted yes, the federal would have used that law to stop them and the instigators of the movement would all have been arrested and charged with inciting the people to revolt against their country., to sedition and betrayal to their country. Those are very serious charges leading to many years of prison for the leaders and the people rebelling and going along with it.

However I never believed that quebeckers wanted to separate they just fought to be treated fairly by the federal and their rights to their language and culture to be respected not having to lose the benefits that the federal can bring them.

So now you know you have a big fight ahead of you and I want you to promise me you won't stop until you have justice. Remember you lost all the goods your parents left you. Only that should keep you going, plus all your souvenirs of a lifetime. You have to promise me you will go on until the end even if it means to go public. My health isn't what it used to be so when I get on the other side I want to tell your dad that you did't stop, that you promised me you wouldn't. I did promise him and that is why i can't stop and give up.

Sadly in 2007 I heard that he passed but my promise still holds for him and the two financial inspectors that lost their jobs for giving me information and helping me.

I was stunned to hear what happened in Spain with the region of Catalonia wanting to separate from Spain who has a no separation of province (or region) law in their constitution. The people were rebelling all over the streets in a big amount. It ended up that the leaders of that rebellion and also many of them being a member part of it are all behind bars for many years with charges of betraying their county. A Spanish friend of mine told me that Catalonia has never been so peaceful.

2005 Appeal Court

As I promised my father's dearest friend I took the disgusting 1995 judgment on the act of sale to appeal, but this time I had all my proof having the mortgage act that I didn't have in 1995. Germaine my friend got me a lawyer member of her association to plead that the acts were false. He did a great job but the judge had an inquisite look on his face all along that my lawyer was pleading at the the end he said that he pleaded very well but didn't understand what we were doing at civil being without a doubt a criminal case.

He said that the acts were definitely false that it was a disgusting human being who wrote them with a twisted mind. He said to my lawyer that he didn't doubt that he knew it was a criminal case and he just didn't understand what we were doing in his court since he is there to judge civil cases.

That is when I got up and told him all my story. He was shocked and said he was sorry for me to have lived such a horror story and that I have to return to the police that it is up to the police to find a crown. He wished me luck, said that he had to reject the case because it was a criminal matter. He also told me that now since I had my whole proof not to give up. I couldn't believe I got a judge that was so sympathetic.

I Took A Break

Having no more possibility at civil with hope that the federal government would change I decided to go help my friend manager of an elderly house who didn't have a cook. I was there for more than six years and found great peace in my heart from helping them and made many friends.

Complaint at the Federal 2011 the federal government changed

When I saw that the government changed I immediately called the cabinet of the Prime Minister. My health was better and I was ready for the fight. I spoke to one of his lawyer who could not believe what I was saying and asked me for my file and my proof. He said they would not be able to do anything about my case but if the law is what I say and I have proof they sure will do anything in their power to have it abolished. I sent my file the September 11th 2011 and the law was abolished the 30th of November 2011. That is how efficient they were. When the law was changed I got a copy of the proof it was sent by Ottawa archives. I spoke to two or three different people of the cabinet who knew my case and told me by letter and on the phone that they did their part with the political party in power in Quebec that they had the law changed but now I had to send my file to the minister of justice in Quebec. They also thanked me for being a loyal Canadian and told me to get ready for a big fight because now they knew everything and that they also were banking all their projects with the same financial system as the political party before them did and they might just decide to try and block my case so it will not be known to the quebeckers.

They told me that they are already in hot water with the Charbonneau Commission that surely they didn't want an other scandal to get out. So I sent my file to the minister of Justice and to the Prime Minister of Quebec. He never answered me but the minister of justice referred me by letter to what they call criminal complaint. They are a department of the ministry of justice where crowns take cases at criminal for people that can't get justice.

Complaint at Criminal Complaint in Quebec (DPCP)

I got a very nice female crown who was disgusted with my case and wanted my documents and also referred me to the person in charge of all the frauds in Quebec from the Quebec provincial police. He was shocked and didn't quite believe my story. When I told him to go to archives of "Carcajou" and pull my file out he started to listen. I told him the name of the investigator who left my file open because I couldn't get justice after the crown refused to act and didn't informe me to go claim my house in criminal court. I told him about the judgement in criminal court in my favour where the judge says that my house should be given back to me. I never got her memo that she says she sent to me and the crown didn't contact me to tell me he got the judgement and tell me to go claim my house. When I confronted him, he said he will not do any accusation against the financial institution that is why my file was left opened by "Carcajou" and why the R.C.M.P. investigation who pleaded against the accused in court told me to tell my crown to send him a subpoena for him to go and plead in court for me.

The police in charge of fraud in Quebec was wordless after hearing all that and said he would go and get the file and call me back. Two days later, he called me and said I was right, that he would organise a meeting with me, my researcher and the police in charge of fraud. He also said he would be there.

In September 2012

The Meeting with the Fraud

I brought a witness with me and thank God i did. We were met downstairs by a police woman who said she was in charge of the fraud. She was chewing gum and gave us attitude. I wasn't impressed!

Just before entering the meeting room where my researcher was talking with the person responsable of all fraud in Quebec, she bluntly turn around to me almost drilling me in the wall and said "Listen to me very carefully Mrs La Gentile, if you think you are here to make a hit on the financial institution, i have some news for you, I can tell you right now it won't happen here I can guarantee you!" I couldn't believe it the guts of her to say that in front of a witness.

Well sure enough she didn't even want to open my file and said there wasn't a fraud. I told her to pull out the acts and I will show her wrong that the acts are fraudulent, that there is a judgment in criminal court to prove it to pull that out also. She was furious and said she simply wasn't doing the case.

Her boss said wait a minute here it so happens I know her researcher from years back when I was at the fraud department we had a case together and let me tell you something if he says that it's fraud I know he has the proof. He took her out for a bit and she came back in furious. He said he was going to put an investigator in the file and she screamed she was going to name him it was her case and her department.

She started to say that she would proceed by interrogating the notary and my supposed partner. I said it's useless do you really think they will admit they frauded me? They denied that in court in 1995. All you need to do is get a copy of the deposition of my lawyer in 2005 in appeal court where he demonstrated how the acts were false and a copy of the judgment in criminal court where the R.C.M.P. investigator proves that it was an identity fraud. The notary put my house to the name of my supposed partner and the judge said she sent me a memo that I never got, to go claim my house. I told her to pull out the acts I would show her where the fraud is because first of all the act of sale says I was paid and I never got the money. The act of sale is contradictory by itself and as if this is not enough the two acts contradict themselves. She was raging and said it was going to be done her ways or nothing and left.

In the back of my mind, I always wondered if that show was not planed by her and her boss because later on, the fraud department did everything possible to kill my case and I remembered what my friend who went to get the law of the financial institution told me after the 2000 hearing in slander of the president of the institution against the president of the victims who had been attacking the financial institution publicly since early 1990.

What Happened After
The Hearing in 2000

As I said before the person who got the law and brought to me was always in contact with me on a regular base so was the president of the victims but I never heard from them after the hearing. I decided to call the president of the victims but his phone was always on the answering machine and I left many messages and he never called back. So I called the one that brought me the law and he was very strange with me. After questioning him for a while he told me what happened but made me promise I didn't say a word because he wanted to live a little longer having not only a bad heart condition but telling me what happened after the hearing.

It so happens that the judge concluded the case by an arrangement out of court. But the president of the victims agreed to be settled for his friend and he asked for my friend with the heart condition to also be settles and an other one who helped him in his cases. My friend told me that the reason he got settled and his brothers in the case was because the secretary who put all cases on internet for the president of the victims asked not to be payed but to settle him in the arrangement out of court being friend with him for a long time.

In the agreement the conditions were to take everything off internet close the website and stop helping all the victims to get to the end of them cases. Also that cut all communication with them, I couldn't believe it how can a person sign a thing like that and abandon all others when he positioned himself as a defender to help them get justice. I was disgusted but I knew I had an enormous fight ahead of me after meeting the chief of cabinet of the political party of 2001-2002 and getting this information I also had been told by the police to leave Quebec because my life was in danger. And now with the attitude of the fraud I was more and more convinced that the two different governments in power one after the other would go to any means to stop this scandal. But still, there was nothing to stop me, knowing that I was dealing not with a democratically government but a "state government" some form of dictature. Later on, one of the police told me that the president of the victims died not too long after the hearing of 2000 and his death was very doubtful. Was he saying that to shake me or protect me because at that point I didn't trust everybody at all level of the Government.

The Investigator of Fraud and his Sergeant

In October 2012 an investigator of the fraud came with his sergeant to question me. The criminalist that was a researcher for the criminal firm in 1999 helped me and advised me all along since he had done all the research at criminal in my case in 1999 for the firm that didn't exist anymore. Knowing my situation with the fraud and mostly with the boss in charge of it he told me to start by showing them the registration titles where the mortgage act is registered to the name of my supposed partner and see what they think. If they don't see the fraud there it's because they have strong instructions by their boss in charge of the fraud department. He said you will know right then where they stand.

So the two came in and I had my friend hidden in the next room to listen to the conversation. The investigator had a sour face, never looked at me but the sergeant was nice, said hello, introduced himself and sat next to me at the table. So I showed him first the titles, after looking at the titles he said it was your house wasn't it? I said yes but he said it's under the name of your supposed partner in the mortgage act, and two days later you sell her half of the house for $112 500 you sell her what? She is already full and only owner two days before in the mortgage act. It's your house and she is now the only owner. He turned to the investigator and said look her house was stolen from her by the documents of the notary. The investigator pulled bluntly the document out of his hand had a furious face and turned around and said "That doesn't mean anything" The sergeant looked at me in a stunned face and asked me to see the acts. All along I was showing all the points of fraud in the notary's documents the sergeant agreed with me and the investigator always found a way of destroying the facts that were written in black and white in the documents.

The sergeant was totally confused and didn't understand from his reactions what was going on.

I knew right then that the investigator had been spoken to by his boss to kill the file and the sergeant was not spoken to. At the end I only spoke to the sergeant and when the investigator asked for the file I didn't want to give it to him only having one and not trusting him with it. When the sergeant reassured me and said he would make a copy and send me my original and gave me his card, the investigator turned around and screamed "I am in charge of this file and it's me you are to deal with!"

The sergeant and I were blown away.

From that day on, the investigator kept my file for more than two years fighting me on all the proven legal points even the judgment in criminal court. He spent all his time at civil in my file in Longueuil to find out later that he emptied it and left only the judgment of 1995 that wasn't in my favour took everything else out and sealed it. When I kept telling him to go to archives to consult the "Carcajou" file and see that there was a note by the investigator to leave the file opened because I wasn't justified, he went and got it and told me it was destroyed because it was too old. There is nothing he didn't do to try and block me from getting justice. Seeing that my criminalist told me to ask him my file back and give me a letter saying there is nothing criminal in my case as he had been saying from the beginning. Since he didn't want to give me one I spoke to his Captain who confirmed me that he had no power to close the file on his own but he would send me the letter I asked for. Later he told me that the investigator consulted a crown of the fraud department and was in no power to close my file on his own. That confirmed that the cover up was now at the police level and the crown of the fraud.

So my criminalist friend proposed me to consult notaries to get an analysis of my acts and all his documents and that he would help me do a denunciation to go in front of a judge at criminal and show all my proof in a private claim.

During that time I contacted the criminal complaint department to inform the crown in my file that the investigator returned my file and I had a letter saying it wasn't criminal from his captain. She was furious, told me to call him back to ask a copy of his police report necessary for her to intervene because without that she can't act. I spoke to him he refused so I call the top boss of the criminal department who was one of the most despicable person. He was arrogant, laughed at me saying I didn't have a case anymore it was closed and no they wouldn't give me a police report. He also said I didn't have a case anymore because he decided and he had the last word not the crown at Criminal

Complaints. But when I told him he would be charged by my criminalist he said to call him in two weeks, that maybe he would do something. Two weeks later, he told me he had the report on his desk but my crown of the justice department won't get it maybe a couple of sheets but not all. When I told the crown she told me to put a complaint at the department of deontology of the S.Q.

So I had my work cut out for me. I had to do a denunciation with the help of my helping criminalist, go and see notaries and call the chamber of notaries for a full analysis of the documents of the notary and once my document was done (denunciation) get ready for a private claim in front of the criminal court. I had to work all day and night but got it all done checked by my criminalist and approved by notaries at the chamber of notaries. I was finishing all my endless tasks and checking everything with the criminalist I got a phone call from the lawyer I was renting my house. He asked me how I was doing in my case, I told him all about the fraud department in my case denying it was fraud and the investigator kept defending the notary trying to convince me it was civil and using the 1995 judgment which was totally false as a defence not to do accusations.

My friend lawyer was disgusted and told me to bring him my acts, the registration on my house and also the acts on my house and the ones on my supposed partner. He told me that is exactly my specialty I have been doing mortgages and sales for more than 50 years if I can't find anything in those documents of the notary to catch him in the wrong, then you can just give up. So I agreed and brought him what he asked for knowing that he had a very good reputation all over the region and I trusted him as a friend.

In 2011 A New Discovery

Two days later he called me to his office telling me he had something very important to show me. He pulled out the registration acts on my supposed partner's house. He showed me where she took in 1990 a loan of $112 500 for investment which was to buy half of my house and then showed me all the other acts and loans on her house that had a registration number but the one for the loan in 1990 for investment on my house didn't have a number. I told him I didn't understand why. He said because that act was never registered. Now here is the act (he pulled it out) and showed me that it was only signed by the notary. So he said it wasn't registered and only signed by the notary because the branch of the financial institution never disbursed the money. That act was put there to mislead anybody checking if the act was there to pay you but since I am an old fox in the domain, right away I saw that the money was never given to the notary to pay you. So if the money was never put out by the branch how can the notary say he paid you $112 500 in his act of sale when the branch never gave him the money?

I was totally shocked, he told me that the notary was a fraud expert but not enough to fool him since he has been in that field all his life. So he said that is your whole proof without a doubt at criminal and with that the police has no leg to stand on and can't say that it isn't fraud.

The Judgment on My House at Criminal

He then asked for the judgment against the accused at criminal and later told me that the judge in court who said that she sent me a memo to go claim my house has to have had the full proof pleaded in court by the R.C.M.P. that my acts were false. Since the accused got charged with being in possession of a stolen good that means that the notary's acts are false and he did an identity fraud by putting my house to my supposed partner's name. The financial institution stole my house from me by the false documents that one of their notary's did. The branch knew very well that they were stealing your house from you the proof is when they took judgment on your house they registered it to Vanessa La Gentile + all. Not to the name of your supposed partner.

The other interesting point is that the judge says that her mandate is to judge only proceeds of crime in that case and not that lawsuit following it or preceding it. The lawsuit preceding is your case that was already judged by her and pleaded by the R.C.M.P. to charge the accused and she because of that fraud had to tell you to come and claim your house. The following lawsuit is that the financial institution should have been charged of laundering money stealing your house by the false acts of one of the notaries and selling a stolen good. Now the question is was she ordered to only judge the proceeds of crime to protect the financial institution of getting such a charge and automatically opening a door for you to get justice? Would that be the reason why the crown told you "I will not do any accusation against that financial institution" Him also probably getting instructions to protect the institution that is the pride of Quebec not caring about you getting justice.

The next thing he asked was for documents in my file in the Longueuil court house. When I did the person in charge, the clerk of the court called me and told me my file had been embedded and only the police can embedded a file and only a criminalist can go and ask a judge to collect it. So my friend criminalist did to find out by the lady that it had been totally emptied and only the police can embed and empty a file so they most have a lot to reproach themselves to do that. So now I knew what that fraud investigator was doing all the time at civil and why he also destroyed my file of "Carcajou", he himself told me he did. He had orders to destroy all my proof. Having all the proof of the new discovery and having it all in denunciation my criminalist told me to call back the fraud and tell them about the new discovery and for them to reopen my file.

In January 2017 I contacted the fraud to reopen my case.

Beginning of January 2017 I was referred to a team leader of the fraud who told me he was newly named. When I said I had a new discovery to my case proving fraud without a doubt he told me that the law had changed and I now had to ask the fraud department where the infraction occured. In my case it was the fraud department of St-Jean sur le Richelieu He gave me the name of the lady who was the inspector and all the information for me to contact her and send her my file.

So I did. When I talked to her after she studied my file she was totally disgusted and said she passed it on to her commander for him to study it with her and take an appointment with a crown. In April he met with the crown who sent him to the fraud department in Boucherville in their district to treat the file and make the accusations. Being a property fraud done by a notary their district S.Q. fraud department had to treat it in Boucherville.

Not getting any news in August I called the team leader of the Montreal fraud department to ask him for the phone number of the S.Q. fraud in Boucherville. He wanted to know why and he said looking in the computer that a crown of St-Jean had the case. Very bluntly he said he had to make a call and would get back to me shortly.

After quite a while I called back thinking he had forgotten to call me back. Very nervously he said he spoke to the fraud and ordered them to send him back the file because it was theirs. I blew up at telling him it wasn't their file anymore that he was the one who told me that the new law was that I had to send my file in the district of the infraction. On top of it all, the file was sent by the fraud of St-Jean and the crown of St-Jean to the S.Q. of Boucherville in their district and he had no business to do that.

He threatened me of doing an "illicit warrant" to me. I don't even know what that means. He told me he and my former investigator would analyse the new discovery. In the back I could hear my former investigator screaming he didn't want to touch that file anymore. Finally he said it was going to be because he decided it. I said yes so you can close it one more time, and he hung up.

In November 2017 not hearing from him I called and with a shaky voice he said that there was no new discovery and they both closed the file. So I said if there is no new discovery as you say, it means that the two of you already saw that the branch of the financial institution never disbursed the money to pay me. So why don't you do the accusation? He went totally crazy and screamed at me to put my complaint at the notarial board.

Oh! I said because like you, you know that they don't respect the criminal code that says that in fraud there is no time limit. Well they have a law against the criminal code giving you a year after you noticed you were frauded to put in the complaint and your proof. Passed that they don't pay. So the trick like my case and many other is for the branch nor the notary not to give you your proof nor you file and the crown to refuse to court order for your file. That way to try to get a bit of your proof you must go to civil. That is why the crown says it's civil for you to spend all your money at civil trying to get your proof. They hold you there right up to 10 years so your rights at civil are expired and you only have criminal rights left. And still the crown block you and refuses to act to protect the financial institution. For the ones that don't have money they just lose everything and the case dies there.

I was lucky enough that my house was seized for proceeds of crime and I saw it pass on television. The R.C.M.P. investigator referred me to the one of "Carcajou" who told me everything and helped me get my documents because he had the whole file from the branch. I am the only one that got to the end also because I had money to pay all the civil and lived through a big depression with friends helping me.

I later called the commander in St-Jean and told him about the Montreal fraud taking my file away from the Boucherville S.Q. He sent me a letter from the responsable person of the fraud in Boucherville saying that it wasn't the Montreal file but theirs.

I also called the crown and told her that the team leader told me he called her and told her there was no new discovery. She was shocked to see that he claimed a file that wasn't theirs and agreed with me that if he called and said there was no new discovery it meant that they saw that the branch never disbursed the money for the notary to pay me.

And that act of sale says I was payed by the notary. She also says that he didn't call her because she would have asked him if there are no new discovery as you say, why aren't you doing accusations?

Complaint in Police Deontology

The minute that the team leader confirmed at the beginning of November 2017 that he wasn't doing accusations, I sent the November 26th my complaint in police deontology. There we have an other institution in Quebec that is there to protect their members against the people with full proof that have been unjustly treated by the police. They answered me that the police team leader at fraud said that my time of a year allowed to complain was passed. My complaint was from the time I had my full proof against the notary without a doubt not from the first complaint of fraud in 2012.

In 2012 I didn't have all that proof without a doubt against the notary nor my proof of the judge at criminal court in the judgment the judge says that she sent me a memo that I never got, telling me to come and claim my house because the R.C.M.P. proved to her that the acts of the notary were false and that my house by that was stolen from me by the financial institution.

So the team leader lied to them by saying I was to late for my complaint, setting it back to 2012 when I didn't have all that proof and the police deontology believed him and not me, like they have done in many cases so I was told by lawyers.

So now with all my proof I had to find a well reputed criminalist who had the guts to take my case in a private claim after consulting many one name kept coming up from most of them. So I called him and he now has my file and I am waiting to see what he will do with it.

Conclusion

After passing 29 years of my life trying to have all my proof I also found out the reason of all those frauds, all across Quebec. One thing for sure it was only people with money and a lot of goods that got hit. They lasted from about 1988 to 2000. The article of January 25th of the Journal of Montreal in year 2000 is a great proof. The president of the financial institution takes the president of the victims of the institution in court in slander. But having the proof of more than 100 files the judge suggested to protect the financial institution an arrangement out of court. I found out by my friend and an other victim who helped the president of the victims with his files and he is mentioned in the article. In this settlement it was decided that they would settle them with the conditions to close the website, get rid of all the documents. The president of the victims had not to have any longer contacts with other victims and also not to help them at all in any way.

Today, in lawyer it cost me more than $150 000 and I am not finished yet in lawyer's fees and more than $400 000 to live through all that, to finish on disability with friends still helping me monetarily up to $250 000$. I was determined not to stop because I promised the two financial institution inspectors not to stop and get to the end because both lost their jobs trying to help me to get my file and the other giving me all the information to confront the right arm of the financial institution president.

I always had in mind that first lawyer who we (Louise and I) thought was crazy but ended up being so right. He had said that the fraud were all over Quebec stealing people with money to support a separatist government in case a "Yes" was voted in 1995 referendum. He said it was a diabolic plan prepared by the president of the financial institution and his lawyers and notaries to fraud people with money all of them working for that institution to gather up a big monetary cushion in case the referendum passes and the "YES" is voted. In that case, they could support monetary the party and all their projects not having anything to do with the federal they thought. Louise and I thought that lawyer was crazy but he was proven to be right as the years went by. He also said that there was a cover up to all level of the government to protect the financial institution and there was no way that they would let any case win against the institution. He also said that if the government changed the new one of an other party would make sure nothing comes out of this scandal to protect the institution that is the pride of Quebec and all the projects of all parties in power are financed by them. 50

Seeing that I was going nowhere with police deontology I called the office of the S.Q. director. I was told he wasn't in duty, he had been put out talking to that person I found out she knew all about my situation and referred me back to economical crimes for a review of my file and told me a new person would shortly be named as responsable for the department

A few months later, a lady got named after talking with her I realized she knew all my case and admitted that there was nothing she could do because in my case like many others, the crown of the fraud refused to act. Of course she admitted that it didn't justify the behaviours of the police involved in my case but there was nothing to do if the crown blocks a case. I was thankful to see at least one police was honest and I had her on speakerphone for a friend to be a witness to our conversation.

At the end of my conversation with the crown from St-Jean she suggested me to get a criminalist to do a private claim because there was nothing else to do in my case. That is to get a criminalist one on one with a judge at criminal court to show the judge all my proof and all the cover up.

I had all my proof in my file plus the two inspectors of financial institutions that could come and testify for me in court. I also had the proof of the unconstitutional law that the federal party of 2011 had abolished. However as they told me that even if they had the law abolished, they still would try at provincial to stop me from getting justice especially now being in the scandal of the Charbonneau Commission they didn't need an other scandal to come out done by the same party of 1961-1962.

I have hope in this government that we have now that they will do something to help me get justice. They so far seem to be honest. I will send a copy of my denunciation with names of all the people in the cover up to the Prime Minister, the minister of justice and the minister of social security so that nobody else has to live what I lived in 30 years. That is not democratic it is a form of dictature at all levels of the government that could also be called a state government like the government in Germany during the second world war.

After meeting with my father's great friend former Supreme Court judge I promised him to take this situation to the end even if it had to go public so that no other government would try to do this to their people again. Like he said "Evil" has to be denounced publicly for the the guilty to know they didn't get away with it.

I would like to inform the minister of justice of points to be corrected after what I lived in the legal system.

1) As mentioned before the fact that there should not be a limit of time of a year at the chamber of notary when a person is frauded by a notary. The criminal code has no limit of time for fraud and it is the law all across the country.

2) The crown should not have such power to stop a case from justice there should be a board to control their cases so people could have access to then being unjustly treated by them.

3) We know that there is a department in the ministry of justice called criminal complaint but they have no power on the police nor the crown unless the police gives them a police report. If not like in my case they can't intervene because the police refused to give them a report, well they had no power to force them to do the accusations so why are they there?

4) As far as access to information all in my case like many others it is a joke. If you ask for a document like a police report or the name of the crown at fraud who blocked my case or anything else, you get nothing. Everything in "Confidential" Always to protect the guilty and not the citizens.

5) Even in the former law L.R.C.Q.4.1 of the financial institution in question at article 598 it is said that when a person complains of wrong doing by the institution you can ask for the inspector like in my case to get your file from the branch. But when they get it they can't tell you any information to help you get justice. In my case the two inspectors told me everything because they were disgusted by that article that protect only the financial institution in all the frauds they did.

6) The department of police deontology after all the proof I gave them sided with the police and believed them against me with all the proof by documents I gave them. However the police members involved in my case aren't there anymore two of theme were out at their pension, the others sent to an other department. The one that was sent to an other department was promoted by his boss who was laughing at me all along it's a promotion for all he did in my case. That being getting my file from St-Jean fraud that he had no right and lying to the police deontology who having my proof sided for him. His boss had the guts to tell me that's why he got promoted.

7) Last but not least the crown that blocked my file from the beginning has been named judge in criminal court for quite a while now. He also got a promotion for all the damage he did to all the quebeckers who lost everything because he blocked all the cases.

So as you can see all these points at the ministry of justice have to be corrected. That is priority to give back the trust in justice in Quebec to all the citizens. And that doesn't include the farce of the Charbonneau Commission also the unbelievable events ending the "Shark" court case.

Quebeckers have gone through many miseries due to a justice system that was corrupted over the years. It is due time that it all changes to give back the confidence of the people to their politicians. Thinking that quebeckers are stupid is a big mistake, that is why they are changing government in the hope that finally one will serve them justice. Hopefully this new government will.

Post Scriptum

I have done what my conscience had dictated me following my values, my principles and convictions in denouncing all that so that hopefully it will lead to changes. I was thought by my dad that one always has to have the courage of our convictions and hope it will bring favorable changes to better all citizen's life!

In the end it is useless to keep on lying and misinform quebeckers to make them believe that Quebec can separate when we know that there is a law at federal in the constitution of 1867 to stop any province to do so. It has been proven in this text as we have the proof in the case of Spain of late. Furthermore, economically what would we have done during Covid19 without the help of the federal? We would have all died of hunger not being able to support ourselves monetarily. We have to realize that a financial institution in Quebec would not be capable to hold up all of Quebec economically and provide us with all the money to survive.

Quebeckers have suffered enough over all those years. It is absolutely wrong to use their pride for their language and culture to lie to them. They just need to make sure that the federal treats them fairly in every domain without missing out on all the advantages of being a part of Canada.

Lastly, I would like to point out that if you go to any court house and enter the name of the financial institution in question, you will find at least 10 000 cases at civil, most of them criminal cases sent to civil by the crown. I did I got up to 8100. 900 hundred pages at 9 cases a page. I had to go because the court house was closing but in 1996 the president of the victims of the financial institution in question got to 10 000 cases as said before in 2000 in the article of the Journal de Montreal there was an arrangement out of court for 3 cases leaving all the rest of them including my case with no way of being paid for all their lost. What kind of justice is that for the quebeckers? A government is supposed to make laws to protect the people not laws to protect criminals.

Although my life has been threatening three times and I had to move out of Quebec often, I never stopped. There should be more than 20 people accused in my case. If anything happens to me I would see that they are all responsible for the attempt to my life starting with 3 of them that i already have proof for in my file. More than 5 people of the financial institution sold each other out and their boss realizing in what situation they had been putting to. I also have many witnesses to prove it all.

_____

Veronica La Gentile

Important Note

I would like to thank all the lawyers, civilist, criminalists, and constitutionalists, notaries and politicians, judges for their help and contribution. Without them I wouldn't have been able to write this book all legal points stated in this book have been verified by all these specialists in their field.

Printed in the United States
by Baker & Taylor Publisher Services